Fragrance of Glory

An illustrated account of the Ascension of 'Abdu'l-Bahá

Michael V. Day

Dedicated to Ruhy Soraya.

**In commemoration of the centenary of the
Ascension of 'Abdu'l-Bahá (1844-1921).**

**"The observance of this anniversary will undoubtedly prompt individuals and
communities alike to contemplate the significance of that infinitely poignant
moment when He Who was the Mystery of God departed from this world."**
~ The Universal House of Justice

The purpose of this book

The purpose of this book is to inspire us to contemplate the example of
'Abdu'l-Bahá so that we live our lives and approach our death in a way
that would win the approval of our Exemplar.

"Grant, O Lord my God

and my Refuge,

that in my last hour,

my end may even as musk,

shed its fragrance of glory!"

– 'Abdu'l-Bahá (Will and Testament)

ENLIGHTENED ✲ PUBLICATIONS

Queensland, Australia.
www.michaelvday.com
© Michael V. Day 2021. All Rights Reserved.

ISBN 978-0-6488472-3-6

Layout and design: Stephen Beale
Design assistance: William McGuire
Editorial assistance: Keith McDonald
Finance and encouragement: Dr Chris Day

Enlightened Publications and author Michael V. Day are
grateful to George Ronald Publisher for permission to quote
from *Journey to a Mountain*, and to the United States National
Bahá'í Archives, Mr Denny Allen, and the Bahá'í World
Centre (including the Bahá'í World News Service and the
Bahá'í International Community) to use photographs in their
collection, and to William McGuire for the use of a map.

Photographic attribution abbreviations:
© BWC: Bahá'í World Centre.
© USBNA: United States Bahá'í National Archives.
Title page background pattern designed by Freepik.
Decorative borders on pages 16 and 17 and page footer element
courtesy of Vexels (www.vexels.com).

Front Cover:
Depiction of front entrance of
the Shrine of 'Abdu'l-Bahá
(under construction in 2021).
Photo: © Bahá'í World News Service

Back Cover:
Depiction of garden covering the Shrine
(under construction in 2021).
Photo: © Bahá'í World News Service.

Previous page:
Drum of the Shrine of the Báb. © BWC

CONTENTS

© BWC

SECTION 1:
INTRODUCTION

Interior of part of the dome of the former Bahá'í Temple in Ishqabad.

Ever since the passing of 'Abdu'l-Bahá at His home in Haifa in the early hours of 28 November 1921, Bahá'ís throughout the world have gathered to observe a Holy Day commemorating His ascension.

In the Holy Land, they meet and pray in His house and also in His Shrine, which is within the building of the Shrine of the Báb on Mount Carmel but is to be moved.

Elsewhere they gather in Bahá'í Houses of Worship and their associated meeting places, in Bahá'í centres, in places arranged by the community, and in private homes.

The story of the events surrounding His passing is usually recounted at Holy Day events commemorating it.

This illustrated account, published in the year of the centenary of His Ascension, is intended to convey an inspiring impression of those historic days.

In 2019, the Universal House of Justice announced that a new Shrine would be built near the Riḍván Garden, a Holy Place that was provided by 'Abdu'l-Bahá for Bahá'u'lláh.

'Abdu'l-Bahá in Edirne, c. 1868.

WHO WAS 'ABDU'L-BAHÁ?

'Abdu'l-Bahá was the head of the Baháʼí Faith for 29 years, from the death of the Prophet-Founder, Baháʼuʼlláh, in 1892 until His own passing in 1921.

He is regarded by Baháʼís as the Exemplar, the model they try to follow.

The oldest son of Baháʼuʼlláh, Abbas Effendi (1844–1921) took the title of 'Abdu'l-Bahá, which indicates His station as "servant of Baháʼuʼlláh".

Opposite page: 'Abdu'l-Bahá in New York City in 1912.

Right: 'Abdu'l-Bahá's tent in the grounds of His residence in 'Akká, the House of 'Abdu'lláh Páshá.

Far right: Exterior view of the Ishqabad Baháʼí Temple (demolished in 1963).

My station is the station of servitude—a servitude which is complete, pure and real, firmly established, enduring, obvious, explicitly revealed and subject to no interpretation whatever... I am the Interpreter of the Word of God; such is my interpretation."   *- 'Abdu'l-Bahá*

'Abdu'l-Bahá was born in Tehran in Persia. Starting from the age of nine, He accompanied His father in His exiles in Baghdad, Constantinople (Istanbul), Adrianople (now Edirne) and in Acre (also known as 'Akká, Akko and Acco) in the Holy Land.

From His mid-20s, He was the chief administrator of the Bahá'í community, and representative of Bahá'u'lláh.

Appointed in Bahá'u'lláh's Will and Testament as Head of the Faith, He carried out that leadership function from late 1892 until His ascension in 1921. The three principal objectives of His Ministry were:

1. The establishment of the Cause (Bahá'í Faith) in the Western Hemisphere.

2. The erection of the Bahá'í Temple in Ishqabad.

3. The building on Mt. Carmel of a mausoleum marking the resting-place of the Báb and the interment of His sacred remains.

In summary, 'Abdu'l-Bahá devoted His ministry to advancing the Faith of Bahá'u'lláh and to promoting peace and unity by His words and personal example.

© USBNA

QUALITIES

According to observers, and even to many of those who opposed Him, 'Abdu'l-Bahá embodied the three key components of the primary injunction of Bahá'u'lláh on how we as human beings should be.

O SON OF SPIRIT!
My first counsel is this: Possess a pure, kindly and radiant heart, that thine may be sovereignty ancient, imperishable and everlasting.

As this pure (detached), kindly (compassionate) and radiant (illuminating) person, He was the "embodiment of every Bahá'í ideal", the example of how to live.

He knew the station of His Father. He was renowned for being compassionate.

Shoghi Effendi said that "in the person of 'Abdu'l-Bahá the incompatible characteristics of a human nature and superhuman knowledge and perfection have been blended and are completely harmonized".

Right: The Shrine of the Báb, c. 1909.

Left (top): 'Abdu'l-Bahá with a group of Bahá'ís at Lincoln Park in Chicago, Illinois, 3 May 1912.

Left: The path leading from the Pilgrim house to the Shrine (partly seen in far background), c. 1920.

© BWC

SECTION 2:
LAST YEARS

'Abdu'l-Bahá looking westward towards the Shrine from the northern balcony of the nearby house of 'Abbás Qulí.

In the last two years of His life, between the ages of 75 and 77 years old, 'Abdu'l-Bahá was still very active, and radiant.

He met with pilgrims from both the East and the West, giving them inspiring talks, and often accompanying them to the Shrine of the Báb.

The Master would often spend the night in his room on the roof of a house about 50 metres to the east of the Shrine (removed in the 1930s), but otherwise reside down Mt Carmel and towards the port, in what is now called Haparsim Street.

Below left: 'Abdu'l-Bahá approaching His home. The Shrine of the Báb is at top, right.

Below: Cypress grove on the south side of the Shrine of the Báb, where Bahá'u'lláh indicated to 'Abdu'l-Bahá where the Shrine of the Báb was to be built, c. early 1900s.

'Abdu'l-Bahá walking outside
7 Haparsim Street in Haifa, c. 1919.

'Abdu'l-Bahá attended to His correspondence and met with local officials.

He accepted the award of a knighthood (K.B.E.) from the British Government, the citation noting that His advice had been most valuable to the Military Governor and officers of the Administration in Haifa, "where all his influence has been for good". He rarely used the title. He gave time for meeting the senior British officials, who were administering the Holy Land, and many of them wrote highly praiseworthy memoirs of their experiences.

The Master at His knighthood ceremony.

'Abdu'l-Bahá with Bahá'ís at the north-west of the Shrine. Raḥmatu'lláh is in the back row, third from right (white shirt and fez), Fujita just below to the left.

'Abdu'l-Bahá was assiduous in seeking protection for the persecuted Bahá'ís in Iran, and via letters asked the British diplomats in Persia to urge the Government there to protect the Bahá'ís from their persecutors.

In 1920 two Tablets by 'Abdu'l-Bahá were delivered to the Executive Committee of the Central Organisation for a Durable Peace at the Hague. In those Tablets He outlined the Bahá'í approach to world peace.

Far right: Abdu'l-Bahá with Shoghi Effendi (third from left, in light-coloured coat) in front of the house of 'Abbás Qulí. Dr John Esslemont, in a light-coloured waist-coat, is in the fourth row; Fujita has climbed up the tree; Dr Loftullah Hakim third from right, front row.

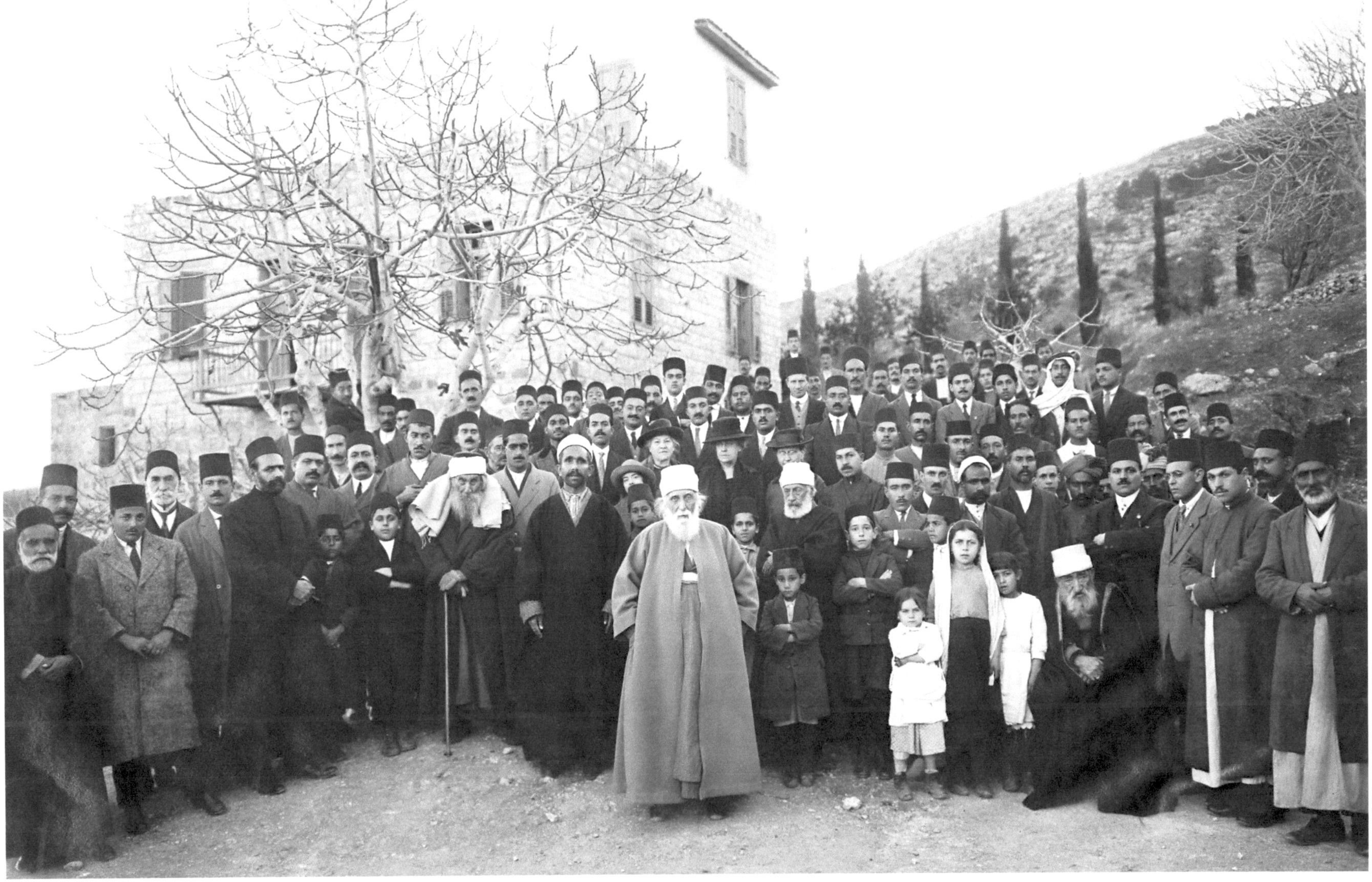

'Abdu'l-Bahá spoke of His wish to visit such places as Ishqabad (now Ashgabat, the capital of Turkmenistan) where the first Bahá'í Temple had been established under His direction.

He also wanted to go to Kashgar, now a city in Xinjiang Uyghur Autonomous region in China's far west.

Other destinations He spoke of were India and the islands of the mid-Pacific.

Left: 'Abdu'l-Bahá walking up Haparsim Street, c. 1920.

Right: 'Abdu'l-Bahá entering the Pilgrim House. Shoghi Effendi is at front, right.

Far right: 'Abdu'l-Bahá on the eastern side of the Shrine of the Báb with Shoghi Effendi (wearing a white scarf, and behind the elderly Hájí Haydar-'Alí). This is a rare photograph of Shoghi Effendi at the Shrine.

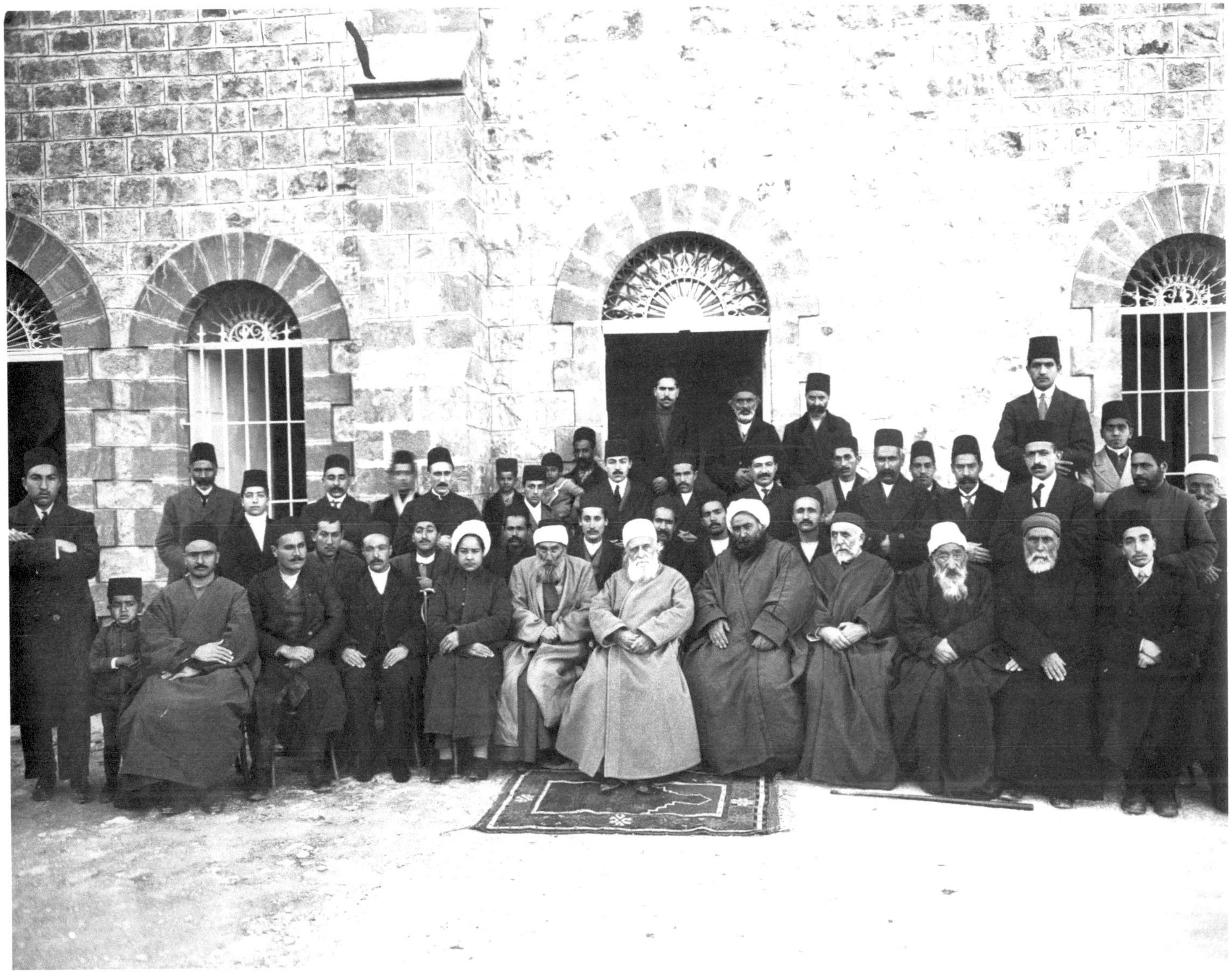

"O Lord! My bones are weakened, and the hoar hairs glisten on My head . . .

and I have now reached old age, failing in My powers . . . No strength is there left

in Me wherewith to arise and serve Thy loved ones . . . O Lord, My Lord!

Hasten My ascension unto Thy sublime Threshold . . . and My arrival at the

Door of Thy grace beneath the shadow of Thy most great mercy . . ."

~ 'Abdu'l-Bahá, 10 July, 1921. (Shoghi Effendi, *God Passes By*, p. 310).

"I have renounced the world and the people thereof ... In the cage of this world

I flutter even as a frightened bird, and yearn every day to take My flight unto Thy

Kingdom. Yá Bahá'u'l-Abhá! Make Me drink of the cup of sacrifice, and set Me free."

~ 'Abdu'l-Bahá, November 1921. (Shoghi Effendi, *God Passes By* pp.309-310).

"O Lord! Grant me a measure of Thy grace and loving-kindness,

Thy care and protection, Thy shelter and bounty, that the end of my days

may be distinguished above their beginning, and the close of my life may

open the portals to Thy manifold blessings. May Thy loving-kindness

and bounty descend upon me at every moment, and Thy forgiveness

and mercy be vouchsafed with every breath, until, beneath the sheltering

shadow of Thine upraised Standard, I may at last repair to the Kingdom of

the All-Praised. Thou art the Bestower and the Ever-Loving,

and Thou art, verily, the Lord of grace and bounty."

– 'Abdu'l-Bahá (Newly translated prayer, 2021)

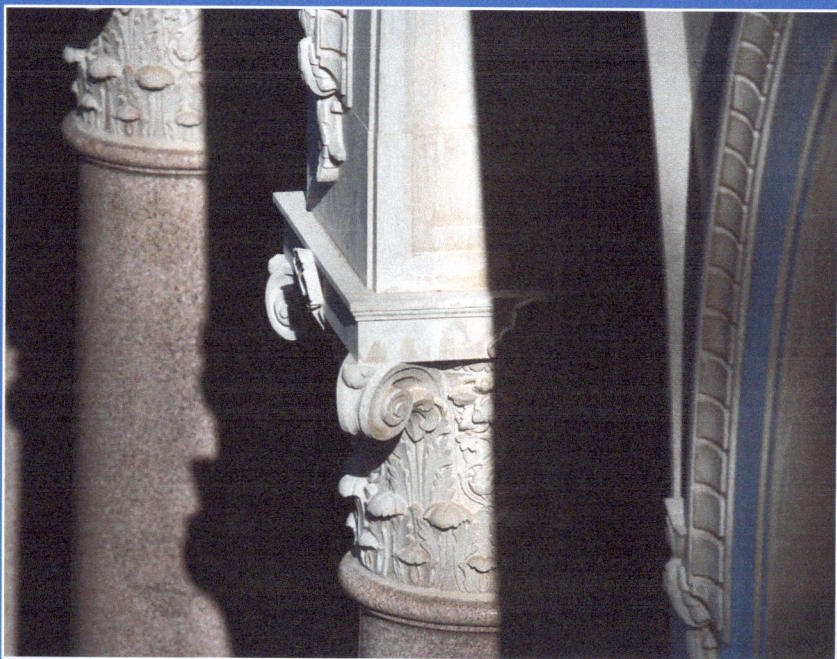

© BWC

SECTION 3:
THE PASSING

Edited excerpt from
Journey to a Mountain.

Detail of the Shrine of the Báb.

On Saturday morning, 26 November [1921], 'Abdu'l-Bahá said he felt very cold and put on a favourite fur-lined coat which had once belonged to His Father. He then went to his room, took off the coat, lay down on His bed and asked to be covered up, saying that He had not slept well the night before. He was feverish in the afternoon, and in the evening had a worrisome temperature of 104 Fahrenheit (40 Celsius), which then lowered during the night as the fever left him. After midnight, He had some tea.

On the Sunday morning, He said He felt quite well and got up and dressed, but was persuaded to remain on the sofa in His room.

Dr Habíb, a Christian Arab physician, gave Him an injection of quinine for malaria. He had been suffering from bronchitis, so may have been treated for that as well.

Above: The interior of the dome of the former Bahá'í Temple in Ishqabad.

Above: Illustration of the Master's room on the roof of 'Abbás Qulí's house just east of the Shrine.

Far right: The room where 'Abdu'l-Bahá passed away.

At 8 p.m. or shortly after, after taking a little nourishment and saying He was quite well, 'Abdu'l-Bahá went to bed in a room on the southern side of the house. His two daughters successively attended to Him because they were concerned about His health. He went to sleep very calmly and was fever-free.

'Abdu'l-Bahá awoke about 1.15 a.m., got up and walked across to a table where He drank some water. He took off an outer night garment, saying: 'I am too warm.' He went back to bed. When His daughter Rúhá Khánum approached, she found Him lying peacefully and, as He looked into her face, He asked her to lift up the net curtains, saying: 'I have difficulty in breathing, give me more air.'

At some stage His daughter administered some remedies that had been left by physicians that day. Some rose water was brought. Without needing any help, He sat up in bed to drink some. He again lay down. When some food was offered Him, He remarked in a clear and distinct voice: 'You wish me to take some food, and I am going?' He gave them a beautiful look.

His face was so calm, His expression so serene, the two daughters thought him asleep. His daughter Munavvar, who was also there at the end, later wrote: 'There was not the least agitation or agony. It was so calm that we could not realize that he was going.' 'Abdu'l-Bahá had quietly passed away at 1.30 a.m. He was 77 years old.

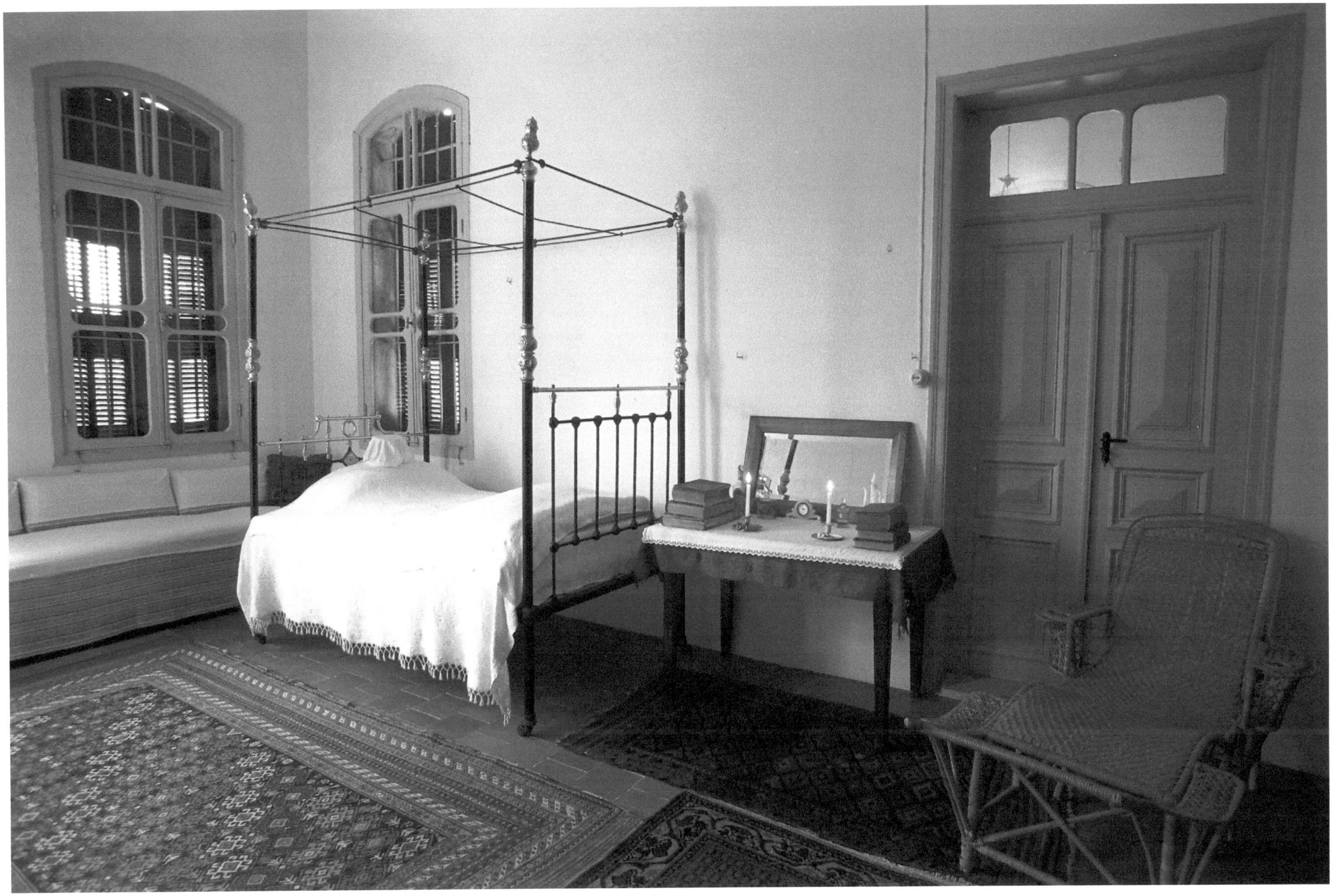

© Denny Allen

SECTION 4: REACTIONS

*Part of the golden dome and drum of
the Shrine of the Báb.*

A medical practitioner from the United States who was a pilgrim, Dr Florian Krug, confirmed that 'Abdu'l-Bahá died, and closed His eyelids. Five other pilgrims were invited into the room. They were Dr Krug's wife Grace, and another American, Curtis Kelsey; Louise and John Bosch (from Switzerland but California residents); and Johanna Hauff from Germany.

John Bosch entered the Master's bedroom and knelt by the bed. Bahíyyih Khánum then took his hand and sat him beside her on the divan that was built-in alongside the window. Munírih Khánum took Louise's hand in hers. There they stayed from two to four a.m.

The mosquito netting was lowered over the bed on which lay 'Abdu'l-Bahá and the pilgrims left for an adjacent room. The door of the Master's room was then closed.

John Bosch recalled that although Bahíyyih Khánum wept far less than the others, remaining dignified and composed, she sighed often during that night and many times said: 'Ya Ilahi – O God, my God!

Bahíyyih Khánum.

23

Curtis Kelsey drove the Master's Ford, with Fujita and another Bahá'í, a servant named Khusraw, in the back, to Bahjí to convey the shocking news to the Bahá'ís there and to call them to Haifa for the funeral.

'Abdu'l-Bahá's sister, Bahíyyih <u>Kh</u>ánum, decided the burial place would be under the central northern room of the Shrine of the Báb.

After 'Abdu'l-Bahá's body was washed, it was wrapped in five separate folds of white silk. A black mitre, given to 'Abdu'l-Bahá by Bahá'u'lláh, was placed on His head. He remained on the bed until an hour before the funeral began.

A white coffin of plain white wood was hurriedly obtained.

On Monday night, the Western pilgrims were permitted to see the body again – the only ones besides the family.

*Above John Bosch (left)
and Curtis Kelsey (right).*

*Far right: 'Abdu'l-Bahá in the Holy
Land, c. 1920.*

SECTION 5: PROFILES

Some Bahá'ís present at the time of the Ascension

Gate to House of the Master, 7 Haparsim Street.

HOLY FAMILY

BAHÍYYIH KHÁNUM. (1846–1932)

The sister of 'Abdu'l-Bahá, Bahíyyih Khánum, was known by her spiritual title of the Greatest Holy Leaf, which designates her descent from Bahá'u'lláh. Her mother was Asiyih Khánum.

So trusted was she by 'Abdu'l-Bahá, that after the sacred remains of the Báb arrived in the Holy Land, He concealed them in her room in Acre for a year.

From 1910 to 1913, when 'Abdu'l-Bahá was away from the Holy Land, Bahíyyih Khánum, remained in Haifa where she undertook a role as the Master's "representative and vicegerent", thereby becoming the only woman ever to hold the reins of an independent world religion. It was a role that she was to adopt again during Shoghi Effendi's absence from the Holy Land. Like the Master, she was fluent in Arabic, Persian and Turkish, and somebody who was much loved by the pilgrims. It was she who decided where 'Abdu'l-Bahá would be buried.

Bahíyyih Khánum

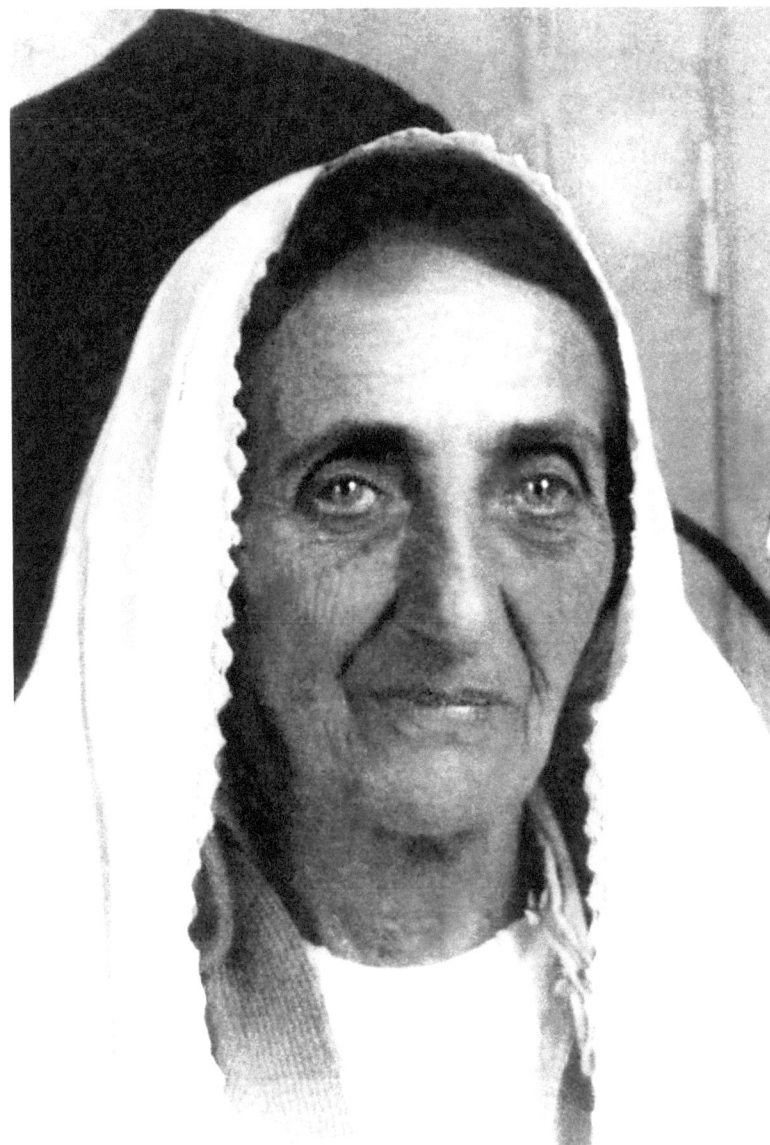

© BWC

MUNÍRIH KHÁNUM (1847–1938)

The widow of the Master Munírih Khánum comforted pilgrims on the night of the passing of her beloved husband.

Munírih Khánum was a talented writer, a poet, an articulate speaker, a teacher of the Faith and an ardent advocate of the education of girls, and perhaps the first Persian woman to write her autobiography.

Speaking to those who knew the Master only in his later years she bequeathed to history this magnificent description of Him when newly married: 'You have known Him in recent years, but then in the youth of His beauty and manly vigour, with His unfailing love, His kindness, His cheerfulness, His sense of humour, His untiring consideration for everybody, He was marvellous, without equal, surely in all the earth!'

Left: Munírih Khánum.

Far right: Dr Florian Krug and Mrs Grace Krug

PILGRIMS

Dr Florian Krug (1859–1924)

Dr Florian Krug, a medical doctor was on pilgrimage at the time of the Ascension. He pronounced 'Abdu'l-Bahá dead, and closed His eyelids. He said he had witnessed the last breath of the Master. At 'Abdu'l-Bahá's invitation, Dr Krug had been staying in the Master's room by the gate of the House with his wife Grace, and had given some medical advice. 'Abdu'l-Bahá was staying in His room inside the house. Born in Germany, Dr Krug had fought 47 duels. He later became a leading New York surgeon. Dr Krug's second wife, Grace, was a Bahá'í but he was to begin with extremely hostile to the Faith. Contrary to his wishes, his wife invited 'Abdu'l-Bahá to their home in New York in 1912. Meeting the Master changed his view of Him. It changed His life. He was thrown into deep sorrow at the death of his beloved exemplar.

Grace Krug (1870–1939)

Grace Krug first heard of the Bahá'í Revelation about 1904 or 1905. She eagerly studied the meagre writings available, and was confirmed in her faith while on a mountain in Europe.

Despite the initial opposition to the faith of her husband, she held regular Bahá'í meetings in their home, and in 1912, 'Abdu'l-Bahá spoke there. Her son, Carl, later reported that the Master told him that his mother would be "one of the famous women of America..... All will know of her servitude." With Dr Krug, she escorted a big group of friends to visit the Master, and after a year in Europe, she went with Dr Krug on another visit to 'Abdu'l-Bahá, in 1921. After the Ascension, she returned to America briefly to bring photographs of the funeral and excerpts of the Master's Will. After her husband's death, she returned to America to once more become actively involved in the Faith there.

JOHN (JOHANNES) DAVID BOSCH (1855–1946)

John (Johannes) Bosch (1855-1946) was born in Switzerland, trained as a winemaker, and moved to the United States in 1879 where he studied the Faith. He received the first of many Tablets from 'Abdu'l-Bahá in 1905. He first met Him in 1912, and was with Him at the Temple site. Replying to a question from John, the Master recommended he gradually change his profession. John did as advised, and developed his properties instead. In 1920 John and his wife, Louise, went to Tahiti as Bahá'í teachers for five months. Immediately after the Master's ascension, John knelt by His bed and then sat nearby with Bahíyyih Khánum. John assisted with the burial and, at the request of Shoghi Effendi, he and Louise took the Master's Will and Testament to the US Bahá'í convention. The Bosch Bahá'í School in California was established after the original school the couple donated was sold due to highway plans.

LOUISE STAPFER BOSCH (1870–1952)

Born in Switzerland, Louise came to New York in 1899. She studied homeopathy. She was introduced to the Bahá'í Faith in 1901. Her first fiancé, William Moore, brother of Lua Getsinger, passed away before they could marry.

Louise obtained guidance from 'Abdu'l-Bahá when she went to Haifa in 1909 with her friend May Maxwell. She cared for May's daughter Mary (later named Amatu'l-Bahá Ruḥíyyih Khánum) when a child. Louise wrote to John Bosch at the suggestion of Edward Getsinger, and in 1914, they married. After returning from their Bahá'í service in Tahiti, she and John taught the Faith in Europe before arriving in Haifa 14 days before the Master's Ascension. After the passing of 'Abdu'l-Bahá, she went with other pilgrims into His room where the Master's widow held her hand. She and John remained in Haifa for 40 days after that event. Louise later devoted herself to the Geyserville Bahá'í summer school.

Louise and John Bosch.

JOHANNA HAUFF (1894–1974)

Johanna Hauff, the daughter of prominent German industrialist, Friedrich Hauff, lived in a magnificent villa in Stuttgart, near where 'Abdu'l-Bahá visited. She is likely to have met Him then. Later, 'Abdu'l-Bahá answered a letter she wrote to Him, and invited her to come to Haifa as a pilgrim. Johanna said she felt treated like a daughter by Him. 'Abdu'l-Bahá asked her to learn Arabic and Persian well so that she could translate the Bahá'í Writings into German. In her correspondence home, Johanna vividly described the events before and during the funeral of 'Abdu'l-Bahá. During her three months in Haifa, she started the translations of Bahá'u'lláh's "Hidden Words". Johanna Hauff returned to Stuttgart in 1922, and continued studying Persian and Arabic, focusing on the translation of Bahá'u'lláh's writings. She married and had two children. Johanna von Werthern (nee Hauff) pioneered to Austria where she became a member of the first National Spiritual Assembly of that country.

Top: Johanna Hauff, later Johanna von Werthern, in 1974.

Right: seated at left with other members of the National Spiritual Assembly of the Bahá'ís of Austria.

STAFF

CURTIS KELSEY (1894–1970)

Curtis Kelsey, a World War 1 veteran from the United States, went to Haifa to design and install electrical systems at the Shrine of the Báb, the Shrine of Bahá'u'lláh, and at 'Abdu'l-Bahá's house. Curtis was a competent mechanic, having worked at the Ford Motor Plant in Detroit. He repaired the Cunningham and Ford cars sent by American Bahá'ís to 'Abdu'l-Bahá but had not been functioning. That job completed, he drove 'Abdu'l-Bahá up Mount Carmel.

'Abdu'l-Bahá wrote to his mother, Valeria, also a Bahá'í, praising Mr Kelsey for his service. After the Ascension, Curtis witnessed the grieving in the Master's house. He drove to Bahjí to convey the shocking news to the Bahá'ís there and to call them to Haifa for the funeral. In later years he spoke about his experiences, inspiring Bahá'ís for decades.

© USBNA

Above: Curtis Kelsey.

Far right: Author Gloria Faizi and Lotfullah Hakim, member of the Universal House of Justice (1963-1968), outside the Shrine of the Báb.

LOTFULLAH HAKIM (1888–1968)

Lotfullah Hakim took most of the photographs now used to illustrate the funeral of 'Abdu'l-Bahá. One report says he went into the vault where the Master's casket was interred, staying overnight until a deficiency in the lid of the coffin was remedied.

Dr Hakim's grandfather, Hakim Masih, had been the first Jew in the world to embrace the Cause.

In 1910 Lotfullah went to England to study physiotherapy and attended the Master during his visit there in 1911. Lotfullah accompanied Shoghi Effendi when he went to study in England. In 1924 he returned to Persia where he served as an assistant to Dr Susan Moody, a devoted Bahá'í physician. The Guardian appointed him to the first International Bahá'í Council, serving as Eastern Assistant Secretary. He also served as a pilgrim guide. He collected and preserved many important documents and photographs.

Dr Hakim was elected to serve as a member of the inaugural Universal House of Justice.

SAICHIRO FUJITA (1886–1976)

Saichiro Fujita, known to Bahá'ís as "Fujita", was born in Yanai, Japan and emigrated aged 17 to the United States, where he studied "practical electricity". In 1905 he became a Bahá'í, the second Japanese member of the Faith. He first met 'Abdu'l-Bahá in Chicago in 1912 and travelled with him in America.

Invited by the Master, he arrived in Haifa in 1919 where he served as an aide to 'Abdu'l-Bahá. He worked on the project to illuminate the Shrine of the Báb, drove the Master's car, looked after pilgrims and beautified the gardens. He translated correspondence from and to Japanese Bahá'ís.

Just after the Ascension, he drove with Curtis Kelsey to Bahjí to alert the Bahá'ís there to the passing of 'Abdu'l-Bahá, and to call them to the funeral. He was in Japan 1938–1955, before returning to serve the Guardian and later the Universal House of Justice. He was much loved by Bahá'ís around the world for his radiant spirit, and sense of humour.

Left: Saichirō Fujita, one of the earliest Japanese Bahá'ís.

Right: 'Abdu'l-Bahá (second from left in carriage) returning along the beach from Bahjí to Haifa, October 1921.

SECTION 6:
THE FUNERAL

Telegrams transmitted the news of the death of 'Abdu'l-Bahá around the world. Winston Churchill, the British Secretary of State for the Colonies, sent a message of condolence, as did the British High Commissioner to Egypt, Viscount Allenby, the general who had befriended 'Abdu'l-Bahá. There were reports in such newspapers as *The Morning Post,* the *New York World* and the *Times of India.*

Sir Herbert Samuel, the British High Commissioner for Palestine, together with the Governor of Jerusalem, Sir Ronald Storrs, arrived by train at Haifa in the early hours on the day after the death.

The weather for the funeral on that Tuesday morning was fine.

The sons-in-law of 'Abdu'l-Bahá and Mr Bosch carried the coffin into the bedroom and placed it on two chairs by the bed. To lift the body of 'Abdu'l-Bahá into the coffin, John Bosch held His knees, Mírzá Jalál held His feet and others lifted His head and shoulders.

Cablegram announcing the Ascension of 'Abdu'l-Bahá.

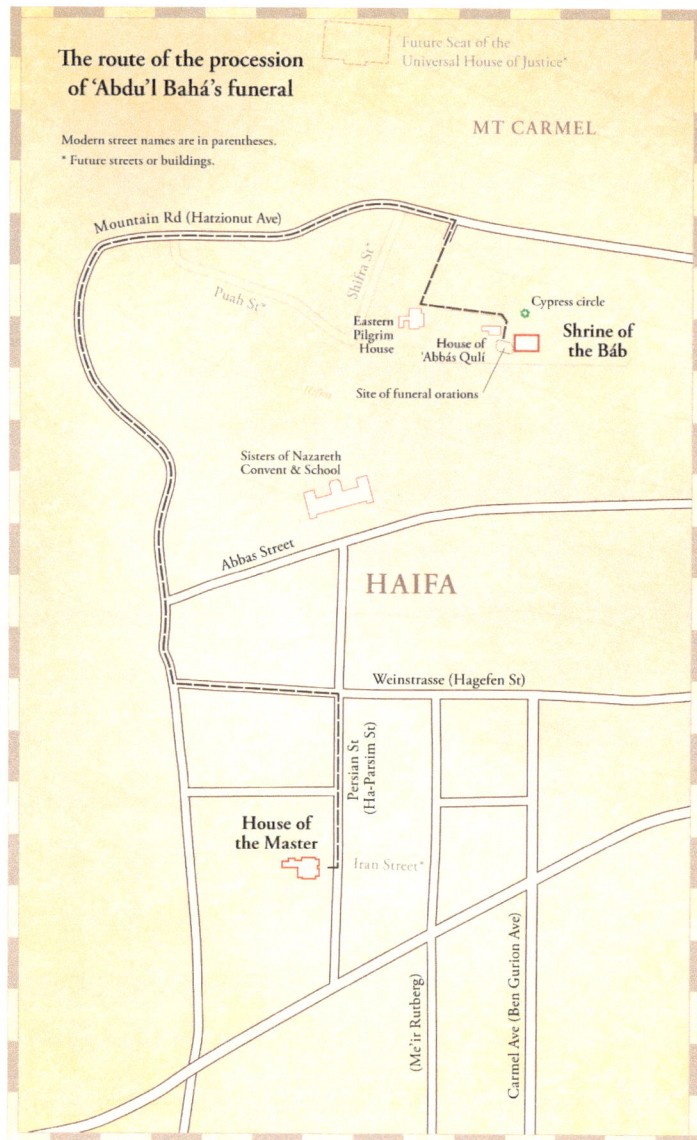

The route of the procession of 'Abdu'l Bahá's funeral

Modern street names are in parentheses.
* Future streets or buildings.

Future Seat of the Universal House of Justice*

MT CARMEL

Mountain Rd (Hatzionut Ave)

Shifra St*

Paah St*

Cypress circle

Eastern Pilgrim House

House of 'Abbás Qulí

Shrine of the Báb

Site of funeral orations

Sisters of Nazareth Convent & School

Abbas Street

HAIFA

Weinstrasse (Hagefen St)

Persian St (Ha-Parsim St)

House of the Master

Iran Street*

(Me'ir Rutberg)

Carmel Ave (Ben Gurion Ave)

Prayers were said in the house. The coffin, covered by a paisley shawl, was then carried out of the house on the shoulders of eight Bahá'ís amidst a throng of mourners. The pallbearers frequently changed during the procession.

Left: Map of the funeral route.

Above and far right: Pallbearers carry the Master's casket down the steps from His house.

Left: Pallbearers carry the Master's casket through the gate of His house.

Below and far right: Crowds accompany the cortège along Persian Street (Haparsim) as the Master's coffin is carried in the direction of Mount Carmel.

The funeral was, Shoghi Effendi was to write, 'the like of which Palestine had never seen – no less than ten thousand people participated representing every class, religion and race in that country.'

The procession up to the Shrine of the Báb began at 9 a.m. Leading the cortège was a guard of honour provided by the City Constabulary Force. Behind them were Muslim and Christian Boy Scout troops, holding their banners and accompanied by their bands. Then came Muslim choristers chanting from the Qur'án. Also in that forward section of the procession were the Mufti (the senior Muslim jurist) and other Muslim leaders, as well as Christian clergy from the Roman Catholic, Greek Orthodox and Anglican traditions.

Immediately behind the coffin were family members and next to them walked the British High Commissioner for Palestine, Sir Herbert Samuel, the Governor of Jerusalem, Sir Ronald Storrs and the Governor of Phoenicia, Lieutenant-Colonel Stewart Symes, and their staff.

Top: Mourners follow the procession along Mountain Road before turning right into the path heading towards the Pilgrim House.

Right: (left to right), Sir Herbert Samuel, Sir Ronald Storrs, Lieutenant-Colonel Stewart Symes.

Left: The boy scouts and police were at the head of the funeral march.

Left: Arrival of the funeral procession near the Holy Tomb.

Following them were, as Shoghi Effendi later wrote, 'consuls of various countries resident in Haifa, notables of Palestine, Muslim, Jewish, Christian and Druze, Egyptians, Greeks, Turks, Arabs, Kurds, Europeans and Americans, men, women and children'.

The cortège came to a halt at a spot a few metres to the north-east of the Shrine. The procession had taken some two hours.

The pallbearers placed the coffin on a plain table, covered with a white linen cloth, in the garden at the eastern side of the building, and the mourners stood in a circle around it.

Then began nine funeral orations of striking eloquence. Colonel Symes also spoke at the funeral. There were no speeches by Bahá'ís.

Sir Herbert Samuel, the first Jew to govern in the Land of Israel in 2,000 years, bowed in front of the coffin as he paid homage. He held his hat in his left hand as he knelt and kissed the shawl covering the coffin, an act repeated by others.

Right: The coffin of the Master can be seen near the circle of cypress pines as the funeral cortège pauses in front of the house of 'Abbás Qulí before proceeding down the path between the house and the Shrine.

Right: The coffin of the Master being carried into the north-east room of the Shrine before being taken into the one behind it and down to the space prepared for it.

Far right: The crowd on the roof and around the Shrine.

Then the coffin was taken into the northeast chamber of the Shrine. Only when the large crowd had dispersed did Raḥmatu'lláh, the caretaker of the Shrine, carry the casket down to the level of the vault.

He placed the Master's coffin facing Bahjí under the south-east part of the central chamber at the north of the building, not under the centre of that room. It was not directly in front of the sarcophagus of the Báb, which was behind the vault wall to the rear, under the centre of the chamber above.

SECTION 7:
ORATIONS

Excerpts

Crowds in front of the Holy Remains
going up Mount Carmel.

The first eulogy at the Shrine was by Yúsuf al-<u>Kh</u>atíb, a well-known Muslim orator, who said in part:

"Whom are ye bewailing? Is it he who but yesterday was great in his life and is today in his death greater still? Shed no tears for the one that hath departed to the world of Eternity, but weep over the passing of Virtue and Wisdom, of Knowledge and Generosity. Lament for yourselves, for yours is the loss, whilst he, your lost one, is but a revered Wayfarer, stepping from your mortal world into the everlasting Home . . . What am I to set forth the achievements of this leader of mankind? They are too glorious to be praised, too many to recount. Suffice it to say, that he has left in every heart the most profound impression, on every tongue most wondrous praise. And he that leaveth a memory so lovely, so imperishable, he, indeed, is not dead. Be solaced then, O ye people of Bahá!"

Above: The Holy Remains of the Master are being carried towards Mount Carmel.

That orator was followed by a celebrated Christian writer, Ibráhím Nassár, who said:

"O bitter is the anguish caused by this heart-rending calamity! It is not only our country's loss but a world affliction . . . He hath lived for well-nigh eighty years the life of the Messengers and Apostles of God. He hath educated the souls of men, hath been benevolent unto them, hath led them to the Way of Truth . . . Fellow Christians! Truly ye are bearing the mortal remains of this ever lamented one to his last resting place, yet know of a certainty that your `Abbas will live forever in spirit amongst you, through his deeds, his words, his virtues and all the essence of his life . . ."

Then came the Muftí of Haifa, Muḥammad Murád, who had spoken with ‘Abdu'l-Bahá in His home just two days earlier.

"This great funeral procession is but a glorious proof of thy greatness in thy life and in thy death. But O, thou whom we have lost! Thou leader of men, generous and benevolent! To whom shall the poor now look? Who shall care for the hungry? and the desolate, the widow and the orphan?"

50

A distinguished Muslim, 'Abdu'lláh Mukhlis, said this:

"I beg your pardon if I fail in doing my duty as far as faithfulness is concerned or if I am unable to pay the generous one who has departed what he deserves of the best and highest praise, because what my tongue utters has emanated from a tender memory and broken heart. Indeed, they are wounds and not words; they are tears and not phrases ..."

After a Muslim poet, <u>Sh</u>ay<u>kh</u> Yúnus al-<u>Kh</u>atíb, recited a poem he had composed, Bishop Bassilious, the head of Haifa's Greek Catholic Church, described 'Abdu'l-Bahá's 'humanitarian deeds, His generosity to the poor, His charm and majesty of mien'. A young Christian, Wadí' Bustání, then recited a poem, which included these lines:

"O 'Abdu'l-Bahá, O son of Bahá'u'lláh! May my life be a sacrifice to one like thee. Thou art the all-wise, and all else beside thee are only learned. What can the poets say in thy day?

O 'Abdu'l-Bahá, O son of Bahá'u'lláh! Thou wert just as God wanted thee to be and not as others wished. Thou hast departed in the Holy Land wherein Christ and the Virgin Mary lived. The land that received Mohammed; the land the dust of which is blessing and wealth . . . We shall be sustained by this Tomb and the One it contains."

Top: The Mufti of Haifa and High Commissioner of Palestine arrive for the funeral.

Below: Outside the Holy Tomb, where the addresses were made by various speakers.

Among the final speakers was Salomon Bouzaglo, 'one of the leading figures of the Jewish population of Haifa, who spoke most eloquently in French'. Here is a translation of excerpts:

"In a century of exaggerated positivism and unbridled materialism, it is astonishing and rare to find a philosopher of great scope, such as the lamented 'Abdu'l-Bahá 'Abbás, speak to our hearts, to our feelings, and especially seek to educate our soul by inculcating in us the most beautiful principles, which are recognized as being the basis of all religion and of all pure morality. By His Writings, by His spoken Word, by His intimate conversations as well as by His famous dialogues with the most cultivated and the most fervent adepts of sectarian theories, He knew how to persuade; He was always able to win our minds. Living examples have a special power. His private and public life was an example of devotion and of forgetfulness of self for the happiness of others . . . . 'Abbás died in Haifa, Palestine, the Holy Land which produced the prophets. Sterile and abandoned for so many centuries, it is coming back to life and is beginning to recover its rank and its original renown. We are not the only ones to grieve for this prophet; we are not the only ones to testify to His glory. In Europe, in America, yea, in every land inhabited by men conscious of their own mission in this base world, a thirst for social justice, for brotherhood, He will be mourned as well . . .

May one not see herein a divine will and a marked preference for the Promised Land which was and will be the cradle of all generous and noble ideas? He who leaves after Him so glorious a past is not dead. He who has written such beautiful principles has increased His family among all His readers and has passed to posterity, crowned with immortality.

'Abdu'l-Bahá (1844-1921).

© BWC

© BWC

Above: Windows on the Eastern Pilgrim House.

Far right: Shoghi Effendi at the time he became Guardian of the Bahá'í Faith, 1921.

SECTION 8: AFTER THE FUNERAL

After the passing of 'Abdu'l-Bahá, a nine-day mourning period ensued.

One of the first descriptions of the interior of the Shrine was that it was 'most bright and beautiful. There are wonderful carpets spread upon the floor and a ten-branched candlestick on either side, besides all the other lights . . . it is all so bright and joyous.'

Because of passport problems, it was not until 29 December that 'Abdu'l-Bahá's beloved grandson, Shoghi Effendi, was able to arrive back in Haifa from England, where he had been a student at Oxford University.

When 'Abdu'l-Bahá's Will was read to him, Shoghi Effendi discovered that even as far back as his childhood, 'Abdu'l-Bahá had named him as His successor. It came as a great shock.

On 3 January 1922, Shoghi Effendi visited the Shrine of the Báb and the adjacent tomb of His grandfather. Later that day, in another place, and without Shoghi Effendi being present, the Will and Testament of 'Abdu'l-Bahá was read to nine Bahá'í men, mostly senior members of His family. In His Will 'Abdu'l-Bahá had clearly and unmistakably appointed His 24-year-old grandson as His successor as head of the Faith, with the title of 'Guardian'.

On 6 January 1922, there was a memorial feast for 'Abdu'l-Bahá, marking the 40th day after His passing, an event in which Lieutenant-Colonel Stewart Symes was one of those to pay tribute to the Master.

© BWC

During the commemoration, Shoghi Effendi led those attending to the Shrine of 'Abdu'l-Bahá, where he chanted a prayer, and later, in the Eastern Pilgrim House, asked the American women pilgrims to sing the hymn 'Nearer My God to Thee'.

The next day, in the Master's house, 'Abdu'l-Bahá's Will and Testament was read in its entirety to Bahá'ís from Persia, India, Egypt, England, Italy, Germany, America and Japan. Whenever the name of Shoghi Effendi, who was not present, was mentioned, everybody there rose in a mark of respect.

Shoghi Effendi was then to begin a ministry of 36 years, during which his achievements were manifold: completion of the Shrine of the Báb; translating the holy Writings into English; editing and writing books; developing the Bahá'í administration; directing the spread of the Faith, meeting with pilgrims; protecting the holy places. Shoghi Effendi did not draw attention to himself personally but his loving charm and deep spirituality and his heartfelt and vital communications won the hearts of Bahá'ís around the world, who regarded him, as he described himself, as their "true brother". He is referred to as the "beloved Guardian" to this day. While in London in 1957, with his wife, Ruḥíyyih Khánum (formerly Mary Maxwell), he suddenly passed away to the great sorrow of the worldwide Bahá'í community. His own legacy is immense.

The roof of the Shrine of the Báb (centre, middle). The small room of the Master's is on top of the house of 'Abbás Qulí (to right of the Shrine).

The Master's successor as head of the Faith, Shoghi Effendi, opened his chapter in his account with Lady Blomfield on "The Passing of 'Abdu'l-Bahá" with these stirring words:

"…The historic Mission with which His Father had, twenty-nine years previously, invested Him had been gloriously consummated…He had suffered as no disciple of the Faith, who had drained the cup of martyrdom, had suffered, He had laboured as none of its greatest heroes had laboured. He had witnessed triumphs such as neither the Herald of the Faith nor its Author had ever witnessed."

'Abdu'l-Bahá (1844-1921).

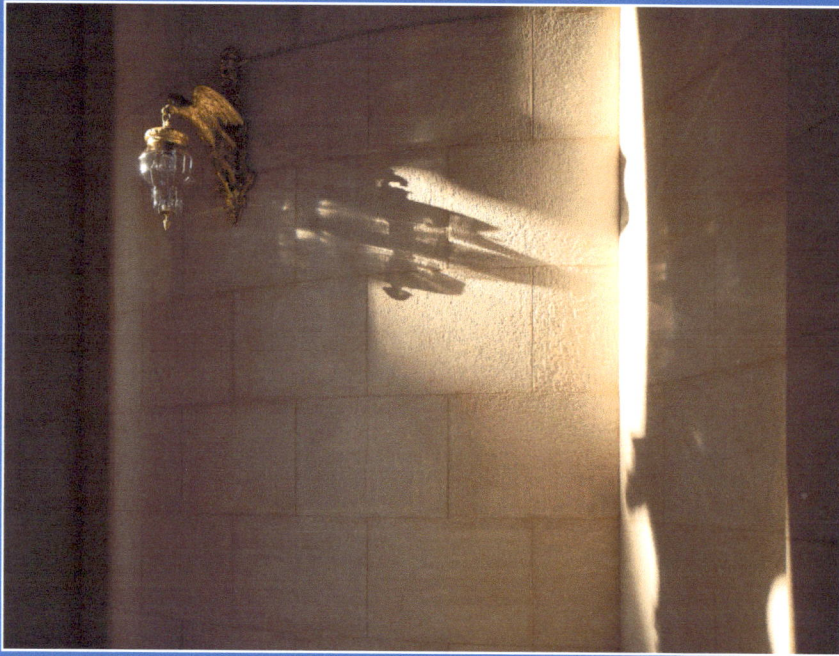

SECTION 9:
THE LEGACY OF
'ABDU'L-BAHÁ

Marble arcade of the Shrine of the Báb.

In the example He set throughout His life and in the way He lived His final days on earth, 'Abdu'l-Bahá left a precious legacy. That legacy also includes His own Writings and the beautiful prayers He revealed. They continue to guide and inspire millions of Bahá'ís around the world. In addition, His achievements as well as the stories told about his life in many books and the record of his talks form part of that legacy. A list of that legacy includes:

A. The Will and Testament of 'Abdu'l-Bahá is a priceless and permanent legacy to humanity, and is described by Shoghi Effendi as "an Instrument which may be viewed as the Charter of the New World Order which is at once the glory and the promise of this most great Dispensation". Among its provisions, 'Abdu'l-Bahá:

1. Names His successor, Shoghi Effendi (1897–1957).

2. Prescribes important details of the administrative structure of the Faith.

B. The establishment of the Shrine of the Báb.

C. The establishment of the first Bahá'í House of Worship, the Temple at Ishqabad.

Shoghi Effendi translating the Master's Tablets, 1919.

D. Establishing the firm foundation of the Faith in the Western Hemisphere.

E. His shining example as Exemplar.

F. His teachings that are highly relevant to the world today.

G. The prayers 'Abdu'l-Bahá revealed, books and recorded talks and conversations. His books include (i) *The Secret of Divine Civilization* (ii) *A Traveller's Narrative* written to illustrate the episode of the Báb. (iii) *Memorials of the Faithful* (iv) *Some Answered Questions* (v) *Paris Talks* (vi) *Promulgation of World Peace* (vii) *Foundations of World Unity* (viii) *Tablets of the Divine Plan* (ix) *Selection of the Writings of 'Abdu'l-Bahá* (x) *Abdu'l-Bahá's Tablet to Dr Forel*.

Left: Entrance to the Shrine of 'Abdu'l-Bahá.

Right: 'Abdu'l-Bahá on the steps of 7 Haparsim Street, the House of the Master, May 1921.

Left: View of the Shrine of the Báb from the road which later became Ben Gurion Avenue (c. 1909).

Right: The Shrine of the Báb just after the completion of its golden dome, 1953.

SECTION 10:
FURTHER READING

*Entrance to the
Shrine of 'Abdu'l-Bahá.*

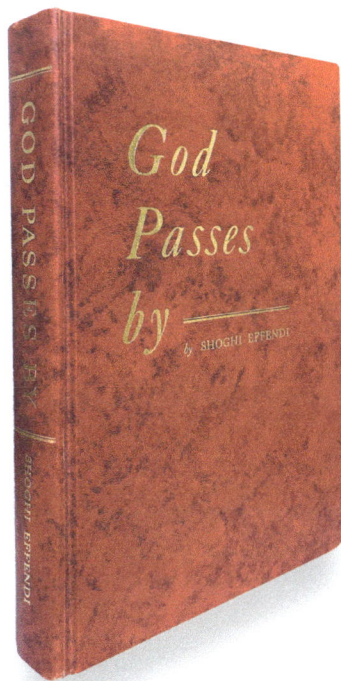

Shoghi Effendi, *God Passes By*, (Wilmette IL: Bahá'í Publishing Trust, 1944), rev. ed.1994. pp 309-20.

Shoghi Effendi, *The World Order of Bahá'u'lláh; Selected Letters* , (Wilmette, IL: Bahá'í Publishing Trust, 2nd rev. ed. 1974), p. 131-9.

Shoghi Effendi and Lady Blomfield, *The Passing of 'Abdu'l-Bahá,* (Haifa: Rosenfeld Bros., 1922), https://bahai-library.com/shoghieffendi_blomfield_account_passing

H. M. Balyuzi, *'Abdu'l-Bahá.* (Oxford: George Ronald, 1971), pp 452-483.

The Passing of 'Abdu'l-Bahá: A compilation. (Los Angles, Kalimat Press,1991)

Michael V. Day, *Journey to a Mountain: The Story of the Shrine of the Báb.* Vol. I 1850-1921, (Oxford: George Ronald, 2017), pp. 120-134.

Earl Redman, *Visiting 'Abdu'l-Bahá: Vol.2 The Final Years, 1913-1921* (Oxford: George Ronald, 2020).

'Night of the Passing of 'Abdu'l-Bahá' by Louise Bosch. Part of a letter written by Bosch to her friends in the San Francisco Bay area recounting the night the Master passed away. http://bahai-library.com/bosch_night_abdulbaha_passing

Robert Weinberg, *Ambassador to Humanity*, (Oxford: George Ronald, 2020).

Angelina Diliberto Allen, *John David Bosch*, (Wilmette, IL: Bahá'í Publishing Trust, 2019).

World Order Magazine, Volume 7, Number 2, Winter 1972-73. https://file.bahai.media/e/ea/World_Order2_Vol7_Issue2.pdf

Twenty-six Prayers Revealed by 'Abdu'l-Bahá: A selection of prayers prepared by the Research Department of the Universal House of Justice and released in commemoration of the one hundredth anniversary of 'Abdu'l-Bahá's passing. https://www.bahai.org/library/authoritative-texts/abdul-baha/prayers-abdul-baha/

https://bahaiworld.bahai.org/special-collections/the-mystery-of-god/

ABOUT THE AUTHOR

Michael V. Day is the author of a trilogy which tells the story of the Shrine of the Báb (see below)

A chapter about the Ascension of 'Abdu'l-Bahá was included in the first book of the trilogy, published in 2017, *Journey to a Mountain. The Story of the Shrine of the Báb. Volume I (1850-1921)*. The chapter was based on previous reports and original research.

Michael was editor of the Bahá'í *World News Service* at the Bahá'í World Centre in Haifa, Israel from 2003-2006.

He is a former member of the Office of External Affairs of the Australian Bahá'í Community (2007-2017), and a former member of the New Zealand Bahá'í Public Relations Committee.

Born in New Zealand, he now lives in Australia. He was a newspaper journalist in New Zealand and Australia.

Website: www.michaelvday.com

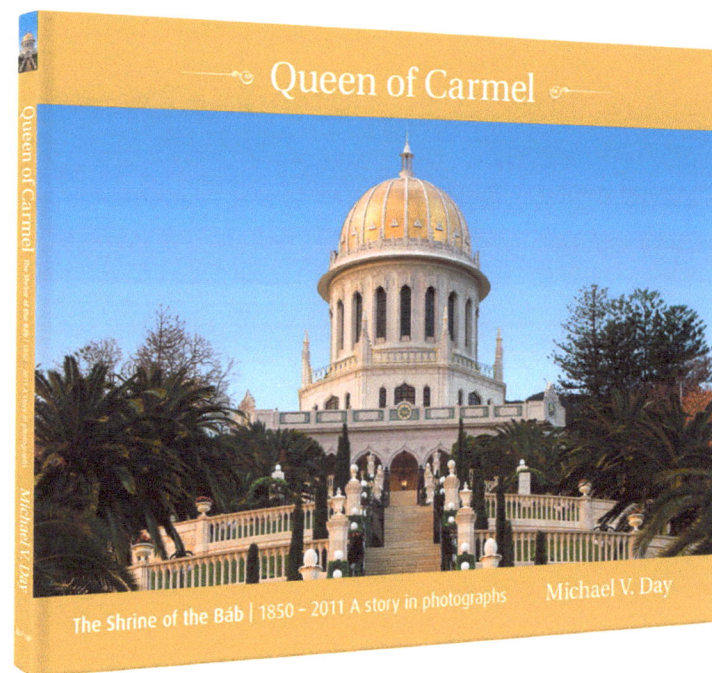

TRILOGY

Journey to a Mountain. The Story of the Shrine of the Báb. Volume I 1850-1921 (Published 2017, George Ronald, Oxford, UK)

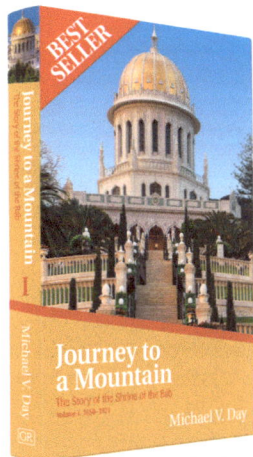

Coronation on Carmel. The Story of the Shrine of the Báb. Volume II 1922-1963 (Published 2018, George Ronald, Oxford, UK)

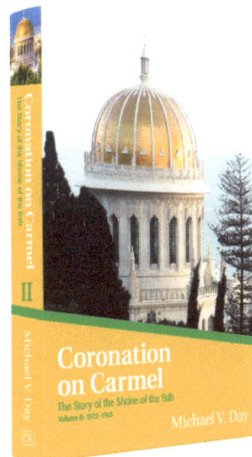

Sacred Stairway. The Story of the Shrine of the Báb. Volume III 1963-2001) (Published 2019, George Ronald, Oxford, UK)

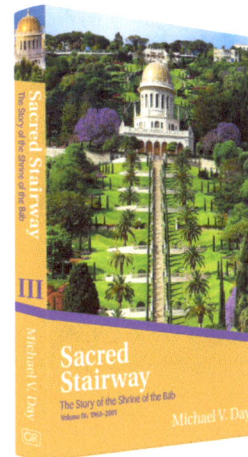

The Shrine of the Bab, which incorporates the Shrine of 'Abdu'l-Bahá (as of 2021).

A decorative feature designed by Hand of the Cause William Sutherland Maxwell for the Shrine of the Báb.

www.ingramcontent.com/pod-product-compliance
Lightning Source LLC
Chambersburg PA
CBHW040711150426

42811CB00061B/1815